Tony Robbins

The Life, Lessons & Rules For Success

D1522970

JACK MORRIS

Copyright © 2017 JACK MORRIS

.

All rights reserved. No part of this book may be reproduced or transmitted in any form or by any means, electronic or mechanical, including photocopying, recording or by any information storage and retrieval system without written permission of the publisher, except for the inclusion of brief quotations in a review.

Table of Contents

Introduction

When President Bill Clinton, talk show legend Oprah Winfrey and Olympic gold medalist Serena Williams need advice, there's one man they call: Tony Robbins. Tony Robbins has it all. The big houses, the beautiful wife, followed by millions and even worshipped by some. He's one of the most respected life and business strategists in the world. But it wasn't always that way.

Coming from a broken home, he decided not to wallow in self-pity and used his less-than-stellar home life as motivation to help others. Over three decades later he is setting an example that anyone has a chance to pursue what they love and nothing should hold you back from achieving your dreams. He's estimated to be worth nearly half a billion dollars today and clients pay thousands, sometimes up to a million dollars a year for his help.

Tony is a master on subjects like health and energy, breaking conventional fears, accumulating wealth, optimum utilization of the available resources, maintaining and enhancing relationships and communication. He was inspired to enter the realm of motivational speaking when he worked under John Rohn who taught him that happiness and success are perception and hard work based.

I'm assuming as you purchased this book you know who Tony is, so now lets get down to the lessons, tactics and mindset that Tony utilizes so well and that we can incorporate into our everyday lives for big results.

The Life

Born February 29, 1960, Anthony J. Mahavoric, now known as Tony Robbins, is an American life-coach, self-help guru, motivational speaker and author. His insights stem from his own troubled childhood. His parents divorced when he was 7 and his Mother followed with a series of marriages. Most notably to Jim Robbins who adopted Tony when he was 12. Jim was a former minor league baseball player who also worked as a salesman. It was a poor household, often struggling financially and unable to celebrate Christmas and Thanksgiving. Unable to provide, Jim left and his mother started to abuse prescription drugs and alcohol. During high school he was elected student body president in his final year and also had a 10-inch growth spurt due to a pituitary tumor that formed the friendly giant you see today. Being the oldest of three siblings he would provide the best he could for his younger brother and sister but at 17 came the breaking point cam when his Mother chased him out the house with a knife. He would never come back, initially working as a janitor and not attending college.

After frivolously saving up enough money to attend a Jim Rohn seminar, Tony immediately found his calling.

He managed to get a job for Rohn, promoting his seminars and filling up the room for him like nobody else could. Possessing a tiresome work ethic and the desire to become rich to help people struggling as he once did, he made his first million by the time he was 24. Two years later 'Unlimited Power' was launched becoming a huge hit and launching him into the spotlight.

With this new found success a whole host of high profile clients followed including Bill Clinton, Oprah Winfrey, Andre Agassi, Nelson Mandela, Princess Diana, Mother Teresa, Leonardo DiCaprio just to name a few.

Costing $7,995 (can vary) for an entry level ticket, his six day 'Date With Destiny' course is attended by thousands of people and has proved a huge success changing the lives of many and more recently being made into a Netflix documentary titled 'I Am Not Your Guru'. This is just one part to the Tony Robbins Empire. He owns a diversified group of businesses in various industries including media production, publishing, education, hospitality and business services. The combined revenue of all these businesses is estimated to reach $6 billion a year. Yes, billion.

Tony owns multiple homes with his main residence located in Palm Beach, Florida. Boasting an infinity pool and a master bedroom that overlooks the ocean he's certainly come along way since his troubled childhood.

He usually starts his day with a dip in his custom made plunge pool that helps boost his energy levels and recover from the intensity of his previous days work. Other daily practices involve avoiding red meat, caffeine and alcohol. His other homes are in Sun Valley, Idaho; Palm Springs, California and the small town where his wife Sage grew up in British Columbia.

Tony involves himself in a diverse set of projects. He has made cameo appearances in the T.V show 'The Sopranos' and the film 'Shallow Hal', both times playing himself. He also starred in Men In Black playing an Alien. More recently he invested in the Los Angeles Football Club alongside Mia Hamm and Magic Johnson. Tony and his partners are building a new state of the art stadium in downtown LA for the emerging soccer team.

Not one to forget his humble beginnings. In 1991 the Anthony Robbins Foundation was created which feeds more than four million people throughout the holidays each year through the International Basket Brigade.

The belief system is that "regardless of stature, only those who have learned the power of sincere and selfless contribution experience life's deepest joy; true fulfillment". The foundation aids the homeless, the prison population, the elderly and the young. The independent charity assessor, Charity Navigator, has given the foundation four stars out of four.

The Power Of Habit

Before we get down to the 'nitty gritty' I'd first like to dedicate a small section to the power of habit. I don't want this to be just another book that you read, get all excited and motivated about, then fail to implement any of the tools or the action required for you to make progress. As the man himself once said, "in essence, if we want to direct our lives, we must take control of our consistent actions. It's not what we do once in a while that shapes our lives, but what we do consistently." So for now, you have to understand one thing—you are your habits. You are defined by your routines. Your productivity, contentment and happiness are, in large part, affected by how you run your life.

And so you are faced with a choice: Do you control your habits or do they control you? You have to understand that once a habit is formed, it turns into an almost involuntary action. Therefore, once you have cemented a habit into your everyday routine, you have little to no control over it. It becomes a part of you and, at times, may actually take control of you. This power can be used for both good and evil. Basically, the formation of a habit is determined by a neurological loop that is defined by the 3 R's: Reminder,

Routine, and Reward. This loop was identified by researchers from the Massachusetts Institute of Technology (MIT). According to their study, the 3 R's of habit will help you understand how a cycle or routine becomes a habit. They can also help you identify the ways with which you can change a current habit or create a new one.

A habit is cued by a reminder, which then affects your action or routine, which then gives you a sense of reward or fulfillment, and so on. In other words:

• Reminder: the trigger that cues your action or behavior
• Routine: the action or behavior itself
• Reward: the sense of fulfillment or benefit that you get from doing an action or by following a behavior

To break a bad habit or to start a new one, you have to familiarize yourself with these three components. You can only eradicate a habit if you understand why you keep doing it in the first place. At the same time, you can only create a new habit if you know what can trigger it and what you can get from it.

You can trick your mind into forming a new habit by using the 3 R's: Reminder, Routine and Reward. But you should also know that creating a new habit takes time. The exact length of the process is unknown. It depends on a lot of different things, including the type of habit that you want to form.

Patience and the 21-day rule

You have probably heard about the "21-Day Rule" of habit formation. A lot of bestselling self-help authors (including Brian Tracy, who wrote books like "Million Dollar Habits" and "The 21 Success Secrets of Self-Made Millionaires," and Zig Ziglar, who wrote books like "Born to Win" and "See You at the Top") have been preaching about this rule in their works. According to them, it only takes twenty-one days to cement a habit into your life.

This "21-Day Rule" first originated from a plastic surgeon, Dr. Maxwell Maltz, who in his years of medical experience has noticed a pattern amongst his patients. According to his book, "Psycho-Cybernetics", it took most of his patients at least about twenty-one days to get used to their new appearances. Having noticed this pattern, he began to observe his own ability to adjust to changes.

Surprisingly, it took him at least about twenty-one days to adjust as well.

However, the "21-Day Rule" is a simplification of the truth.

Dr. Maxwell Maltz did not say that it took a definitive twenty-one days for new changes to become normal parts of people's lives. He said that it took at least twenty-one days for people to be accustomed to changes.

Brian Tracy and Zig Ziglar, among many authors, got this concept wrong. They assumed that the number was absolute, even though it was, in reality, usually the minimum.

So how long does it really take for a habit to stick? Science says the number is 66.

The European Journal of Social Psychology published a study, which was headed by Phillippa Lally, a health psychology researcher from the University College London.

In this study, Phillippa Lally and her team observed ninety-six people over the course of twelve weeks, during which the participants tried to form new habits. The participants chose the habit that they wanted to form, and every day they would report about their individual progresses. They would tell the researchers if they did the routine or not, as well as if the routine felt natural to them or not.

At the end of this study, Phillippa Lally and her team discovered that it took an average of sixty-six days before new routines turned into habits. (Take note of the word average.) In reality, the length of the process of habit formation ranged from eighteen to two hundred fifty-four days. Phillippa Lally

---

concluded that, in general, it will take a person two to eight months before new habits can form.

There is another important finding in this research study. Over the course of twelve weeks, some participants failed to do their desired habits every single day. This, however, did not hinder them from forming the habit in the long-run. Therefore, the process of habit formation is not necessarily about perfection. You can mess up once in a while, and it will not have a significant effect on the formation of your desired habit.

So it takes about sixty-six days to form a habit. During this time, you may stumble and fail, but the important thing is that you keep trying. Again, patience is an important part in the process of habit formation. If you have not formed a habit within twenty-one days, it is not a problem. Neither can most of us. That being said, for some of you lucky people a habit formation will take less than 21 days. We're all different so just focus on bettering your self each day and not comparing progress to others.

Priming

"I made a deal with myself: If you don't have 10 minutes for yourself, you don't have a life,"

What if you could start every single day exactly like Tony Robbins?

What would you do? What would you achieve? How would you feel? Now you can find out. The following is Tony's 10-15 minute morning ritual he uses to kick start the day. Just taking the time and enforcing the discipline to form this habit will dramatically improve your day, week, month and year. He refers to this routine as 'priming' for the day ahead and its purpose is to condition your mind, body and emotions to bring out the best in you right from the minute you wake up. **Start your day extraordinary.**

Wake up. Feel the cold

Although not specifically part of the priming routine, this is the first thing Tony does upon waking.

Regardless of how much sleep he got or where he is in the world he says nothing can change kick start your system like a radical change in temperature. If he is based at his home in Florida, this means jumping into his plunge pool, if in Idaho, going for a dip in the freezing River outside of his home. Tony likes to jump straight in and emerge himself for a minute straight. You may be saying to yourself you don't have access to these types of facilities but if you're reading this, I'm sure you have access to a shower with cold water. Start small, take your morning shower and just turn the water cold for the final 20 seconds and slowly build up. You will come out feeling invigorated and energized I assure you. There is also plenty of science behind cold exposure that I won't go too deep into but the cold causes a release of Norepinephrine. Norepinephrine is a chemical released from the sympathetic nervous system and produces the subsequent benefits of definite energy increase, clarity of mind, and overall feeling of well-being. Now onto the actual "priming" that can be broken down into three parts. Some type of instrumental meditative music can be played throughout.

Part one: Breathing exercise

The aim here is to gain control of your physiology and ensure alignment with yourself. This ritual involves powerful and directed breathing and movement to center yourself so that you're primed for whatever the day brings. First do three sets of Kapalabhati Pranyama breaths. This is an ancient yoga exercise and although it may sound complex it is actually quite simple after some consistent practice. The main point to remember whilst performing this exercise is that your inhale should be passive but your exhale is the forceful movement. As with the cold exposure, start slow and steadily build some speed if you feel comfortable to do so.

• Get comfortable and sit in an upright position whilst resting your hands on your stomach

• Take a full deep breath before you begin, in through your nose and out through your mouth.

• Fill your stomach to roughly 75% capacity inhaling through the nose

• In a quick burst, forcefully expel all the air from your lungs whilst pulling your navel in towards your spine. You want to be primarily using the diaphragm.

• Using no effort, now allow your lungs to fill up naturally and repeat.

Personally, I prefer to see an exercise in action before attempting it so if you feel like you need any further clarification for this just search on YouTube for a demonstration and plenty of quality tutorials are available. As to why Tony does this? This improves his breathing and energy levels throughout the day and also changes the way he moves in a positive manner.

Part two: Express gratitude

Tony constantly expresses focusing on fulfillment over achievement. The whole point is to enjoy the journey and not to just focus on the destination. The key to fulfillment is gratitude. He also mentions "The reason I picked gratitude is because when you're grateful you can't be angry or fearful." He will then take a few minutes to think of three things he's grateful for. These don't have to be big things as examples he gives are the feeling of wind on his face or the smile of his son. This can also be done in a two-part step:

- Current: For the first minute, focus on what you are grateful for to currently have in your life. This is where many people go wrong focusing only on what they want and not recognizing how much they already have.

- Future: That being said, it is always important to have goals and plans for the future life you would like to work towards. For the second minute, focus on your future and what you will be grateful for when you receive it. Through this constant visualization you will build a certainty in your mind about the way your future will look and it will be much easier to work towards. Remember that everything we create in life, first started out as a thought.

This stage is especially important to ensuring lasting happiness. No matter how rich or 'successful' you become, if you're not grateful, you're miserable. If we flip that around, when you're grateful, you automatically become rich. Maybe not financially initially, but there is more than one route to happiness. Give yourself the gift of gratitude.

For many it can be hard to come up with three new things every day, just remember they can be as big or as small as you like and if you are still struggling here are some ideas Tony offers up:

- Who do you love?

- Who loves you?

- What happy memories do you have?
- What is the wealth you have currently in your life – friends? Ideas? Books? A roof over your head?
- What's right in your life?
- What can you see that is beautiful?
- What can you feel that is magical?

Part three: Pray & incantations

The final part, although titled 'Pray' does not have to be tied to religion. Take a few minutes to simply wish good things on yourself and others or seeking strength is completely fine. This is supposed to be a spiritual exercise and is also meditative. This is also a good time to state your incantations. For those of you who don't know what these are, Incantations are empowering phrases or language patterns that you verbalize loudly and with absolute certainty. When using these, it is more powerful not to just verbalize, but to use your body and voice. The combination will change your physiology and your state and this can change everything. An example Tony uses at one of his events that you too can use:

NOW I AM THE VOICE.

I WILL LEAD NOT FOLLOW.

I WILL BELIEVE, NOT DOUBT.

I WILL CREATE, NOT DESTROY.

I AM A FORCE FOR GOOD.

I AM A FORCE FOR GOD.

I AM A LEADER.

DEFY THE ODDS.

SET A NEW STANDARD.

STEP UP!

Remember, incantations are expressed preferably out loud with emotional energy, intensity, and conviction. Many find more powerful results when standing, jogging or even working out. Have fun with it and try to come up with your own incantations to suit your goals.

Post priming

Once he's done with his rituals, he'll typically go for an unexciting but nutritious breakfast, usually fish and salad. He self admittedly keeps food 'boring' as he just views it as fuel with no emotional attachment.

Then it's off to win the day.

35 Life Changing Quotes

Choose To Become Something More

"Life is a gift, and it offers us the privilege, opportunity, and responsibility to give something back by becoming more."

It is easy to forget the gift of the present, of life itself. The very fact that we exist; that we are alive is a blessing. For as long as we are living, we have the opportunity to create something meaningful no matter how difficult our present circumstances seem to be.

Anthony Robbins did not have an easy childhood. His father left and his mother succumbed to drug addiction and alcohol abuse. From a very young age, he had to rely on himself. His siblings also relied on him. Out of his chaotic and abusive home life, he pushed himself to become something more, and he continues to do so because he knows that the best way to become a productive member of the society is to make something better out of his life.

Life can be so unfair and difficult. It is up to you whether to remain stuck in a rut or find the courage to become who you want to be. Dare to dream. Look past your present circumstances. Allow yourself to envision something better. So how do you become something more? You can start with the following suggestions:

Reflect

Slow down and look into your life. Find peace in quietness. It is in the quiet moments that we often find the answers that we have been looking for. Listen to yourself and quiet the external noise. A simple activity such as taking daily walk in nature, jogging around the park, sitting quietly in a bench or yoga can help with self-reflection.

Dare to change your story

More often than not, we limit ourselves to what we know and focus on. We focus too much on the negative things about ourselves, about whom we are, the things we are capable of doing and the things we think we deserve. We tell ourselves, "I am not good enough" or "I do not deserve this." If we can get past these self-limiting thoughts, then it will be easier for us to turn a chapter and rewrite our stories with courage and confidence. This makes us capable of taking action and turning that story into reality.

Embrace your uniqueness

Yes, we all have our share of weaknesses. We are flawed beings. However, each of us have something great to offer to the world. When we learn to accept our own set of talents, skills, strength, creativity and knowledge, we are able to appreciate our worth. Own your uniqueness. There is nobody like you in the world so be damn proud!

Build your confidence

If you continue to tell yourself you can't, you will never believe that you can. Failure is part of life. Everybody fails more than once. If you are too scared to take a chance, you will never know what could have been. Encourage yourself through positive affirmations. Create a vision board. Focus on all the things you want to achieve.

Dare To Change

"We can change our lives. We can do, have, and be exactly what we wish."

At the age of 17, Tony ran away from home after being chased by his mother with a knife. He never stepped into their house again. To survive, he worked as a janitor. And yet without a college education, he became a well-known author inspiring countless of people to make their lives better. He became a wealthy businessman and a respected philanthropist. As a matter of fact, he made it to Forbes magazine's "Celebrity 100."

Believe in yourself
Whatever it is that you want to become or whatever it is you want to achieve, remember that you have the power to make it happen. You can do what you wish. You can have everything your heart desires, but the most important thing is that you believe in yourself. Believe that you can make it happen.

Figure it out

What is it that you want to be? What do you want to achieve in your life? What do you want to be known for? What is the legacy you want to leave behind? How do you want to be remembered?

You must figure it all out first. Identify what you are passionate about. Feel strongly about it.

Determine what you can do now

Success is a step-by-step process. Overnight success is not realistic. However, once you have figured out your vision for your life, it is easier to draw out a plan to turn it into reality. What you can do now may not necessarily give you all the things you want at once. However, what you do right now will bring you one step closer. Determine these actions, and make sure to follow through.

Set Your Goals

"Setting goals is the first step in turning the invisible into the visible."

For many people, the idea of the future is so far-fetched. It is not as real as the things of the past and the experiences in the present. They feel so disassociated with their concept of their future self. Do not make the same mistake. Although it may take time before you attain the full realization of your personal vision, know in your heart that every small step you take today towards your goals confirms your vision of your future self that is manifesting in the present.

For a kid with an unpleasant childhood, Anthony Robbins managed to become something and someone. There are many others who suffered through early setbacks in life but it is what you do with your unfortunate circumstances that matter. Is it realistic to expect a janitor to go on to earn $30 million a year? Do you think it is possible for someone without a college education or background in psychology to come up with groundbreaking self-help books? Tony Robbins is living proof that it is indeed possible.

Find something personal

What is it that matters to you? How do you plan to live your life? What are the things that give your life true meaning? Effective goals are deeply personal.

You have to stop thinking about other people's expectations of you

Today is as good a time as any to stop thinking about how society defines success. Your life is your own. Make sure that it is all about you. Be open and honest. Do not allow yourself to be restricted by other people's expectations about how you should live your life and what you need to work towards.

Be precise

Go through specific aspects of your life that you want to focus on. Do not just write, "I want to be healthier" or "I want to be rich" or "I want to be a better parent or partner." If you want to be healthy, visualize what being healthy means to you and add in solid numbers like wanting to be a certain amount of weight lighter. If you want to do better financially, visualize your dream house or your dream lifestyle and write down the specific weekly, monthly or annually figure you desire.

Make Your Goals Magnetic

"Goals are like magnets. They'll attract the things that make them come true."

Tony Robbins' success came with plenty of challenges, but he figured out clearly what he wanted and found ways to make them happen. His life is guided by goals every step of the way. How do you set magnetic goals?

It is not just about setting goals, though. Your goals must be effective to drive you to action. Effective goals have five major characteristics - specific, measurable, attainable, relevant and time-bound.

Effective goals are specific

When you create your goal statements, make sure that you answer these questions: what, who, where, when and how. Be specific about what you want and how you plan to make it happen. There has to be a clear end sight and the "how to get there" is your assurance that you can do something now to reach it.

For instance, if you want to build your career, you cannot simply say, "I want to work harder". Instead, you can say, "I am getting a promotion in a year's time by being more proactive in taking on more projects, building teamwork with other department members and acquiring new skills by taking classes." This career goal is still a little broad. You can break it down further.

Clear goals are measurable
Realizing your vision and reaching your goals is a process. It may even take a lifetime to achieve your vision, but you can certainly work towards it through yearly, monthly, weekly and daily goals. In other words, make sure to have a measure for success. Include what it is that will make you say you have completed your objective.

Smart goals are attainable
What are impossible goals? For instance, targeting a 60-hour work week is insane. It may be doable for some but it doesn't come with a price. We only have 24 hours in a day. How many hours of sleep will this get you and also considering you have other activities to attend to? Targeting a promotion in six months time is impossible when you are hoping for an executive position that usually takes at least a year to happen.

Cut yourself a little slack. Do not make it too impossible that you are only setting yourself up for failure. However, avoid making it too easy either that it doesn't challenge you to do better. Strive for effort. You will be pleased and proud with yourself for achieving something that you work hard for. It will provide you with a sweet sense of satisfaction. It will boost your confidence in taking on challenging goals. It will drive you to improvement.

Effective goals are relevant

We all have the tendency to please. Realize that it is impossible to please everyone and you don't have to because what matters the most is that you are pleased with yourself. Stop trying to impress others. Instead, work on impressing yourself. Quit depending on other people for approval. Avoid trying to meet their expectations.

At the end of the day, what matters is how you feel and think about yourself. It is your time and energy you are using. Spend it on what is most important to you. Make it personal and relevant. If a goal does not mean much to you, you are more likely to not follow through.

Clear goals are bound by time

Another crucial element of goals is a deadline. It must have a beginning and an end date. This is important not just because it allows you to create a plan around achieving your goal. It is also a way of measuring your progress.

While deadlines are not necessarily pleasant, they work effectively in instilling a sense of urgency in us. Putting a limit on time is also a reminder of how valuable it is. Most importantly, what a specific target does is it pushes us to take action.

Remember these pointers. Write down your goals with this guide in mind. Make them more tangible on a piece of paper. Finally, avoid bombarding yourself with more goals than you can handle. If possible, work on one or two goals at a time.

Concentrate Your Power

"One reason so few of us achieve what we truly want is that we never direct our focus; we never concentrate our power. Most people dabble their way through life, never deciding to master anything in particular."

The smartest people in the world do not necessarily know everything about all things. Rather, they know a lot about certain things. The most successful people in the world do not attempt to do all things. Rather, they focus their efforts on mastering a few things. That is exactly what Tony Robbins did.

After working for Jim Rohn, Robbins learned quite a lot. He worked like a sponge, absorbing everything he could and used the things he learned over the years to build his own brand on the route to becoming a successful health coach. He trained with the best people including John Grinder, the co-founder of NLP or neuro-linguistic programming. He taught himself Ericksonian hypnosis and strived to master NLP. He knew what he wanted and focused on improving himself so he could become the man he envisioned.

All things are not created equal. There are just some things that are more essential than others. This is basically what the 80/20 principle otherwise known as 'pareto's law' tells us. Eighty percent of the outcome comes from twenty percent of effort. Focus only on what is essential.

Take a short cut

Most of the time, you don't necessarily have to take the full course mastering all areas. Taking a short cut can save you time to get the more important things done. Remember the 80/20 rule. Become more selective about where you focus your efforts. Choose wisely the things you invest your time and resources on.

Be a master of something

A lot of people brag about becoming a jack-of-all-trades. There is no point in becoming good at everything if you haven't truly mastered at least something. Stick to a few things and do your best in them. The smartest people in the world rarely know everything. Rather, they have mastered one or two areas.

Redirect Focus Away From Fear

"Focus on where you want to go, not on what you fear."

In 1983, Tony Robbins worked on learning to walk through fire. Before that, he learned skydiving and trained himself for board breaking. And these are not pointless pursuits. But why is this important? It has something to do with fear and it indeed was the best way to demonstrate the fact that fear is immaterial. It is all in the mind as long as you train yourself to push through it, you can conquer anything.

Improve your willpower through imagination
Imagination is such a powerful thing. Our worries and fears are born out of imagination. In the same way, you can utilize imagination in a positive way. The human body responds to situations in the mind in a similar way as it does to real life experienced situations.
When you imagine something bad happening like messing up a business presentation for instance, you will start to feel

sweaty and tense. On the other hand, if you imagine being in your favorite place like resting on the beach perhaps and enjoying the cool breeze and calming sound of the waves, your body will start to relax. You just have to find a way to use your imagination to your best possible advantage.

Replace your thoughts

There are thoughts that fill us with dread. They may not be real but thinking about them makes them feel real, but here's the deal. You own your thoughts. It is one of the things you have control over. Whatever that dreadful thought is that gives you anxiety, through constant practice you can actually train your mind to think of something much more pleasant.

Attitude Of Gratitude

"When you are grateful, fear disappears and abundance appears."

How can you make something out of nothing? How can you get out of the rut that you're in? When a person knows nothing else but pain and suffering, fear becomes too strong. With fear, hope dies.

Tony Robbins could have given up easily early on but he didn't. That's because he knew, even then, how to appreciate the things he had although he had very little.

Choose to be grateful

One of the things that can tone down the stress and help you adopt an optimistic outlook is to practice gratitude. You can wake up grumpy every day dreading what is ahead or you can choose to be thankful and feel good about the things and people you are blessed with. How to do this is documented in the priming chapter.

What about taking the 10 extra minutes in bed thinking about how thankful you are to have had a nice bed to sleep in, another day to live, another opportunity to make things better, more time with the people you care about, having a job, having some food in your kitchen, having a roof over your head, etc? What about getting everyone in the family involved by saying a little thank you for breakfast on your table?

Strive For Mastery

"Most people have no idea of the giant capacity we can immediately command when we focus all of our resources on mastering a single area of our lives."

It was not until he began training with Jim Rohn that Tony figured out his true passion. Rohn was his mentor. It was Rohn who taught a young Tony the value of hard work and perception, its impact on success and happiness. Since then, Tony did everything he could, focused his energy, spent his time wisely and used his resources to teach himself all the things he needed to pursue the career he desired.

Define your vision of your future self.
What kind of person do you want to be? What do you have to do to meet these needs in a more productive way? How should you live your life?

Choose your mission
The thought of a mission can be scary. It seems to be such a

huge concept that not everyone can handle. However, if you really think about it, it is not so difficult to define. A clear mission statement must answer the following questions.

What are the things that I want to do?

Who are the people I want to help?

What value will I be able to create?

What is the outcome I am aiming for?

This is certainly worth spending time on.

Choose a mission that is not just beneficial to you. It must be personal but you also need to think about what good it will provide for other people and the rest of the world to truly feel positive about it.

Focus Your Energy

"Where focus goes, energy flows."

Choose your path carefully

Careers are hard to build. It takes time, but it all starts with carefully choosing which direction to choose. A job is not just a job. An employer is not just another item to list in your resume. These choices matter. Path 'A' and path 'B' can lead to drastically different outcomes. In either case, you must choose carefully.

Follow your passion

It is also important to emphasize the importance of choosing to do things that you feel passionate about. Passion is fuel to motivation. Money can be an effective motivational tool but unless you genuinely enjoy what you're doing, the motivation won't last.

Try A Different Approach

> "If you do what you've always done, you'll get what you've always gotten." – (Henry Ford, quoted by Tony Robbins)

How will you encourage people to push through their fears? For Tony Robbins, it was doing something bold and different. It also required him to take a risk. He started getting positive attention as he integrated fire walking into his seminars. His unique approach to self-help along with his inspiring books made him a great success.

Try a different approach for once

The lesson here is to start doing things differently. If you try the same approach a hundred times, you're likely to get the same result. Your present circumstances are a result of your decisions and actions you may have or have not taken over time. If you want things to change, you have to be prepared to do thing differently.

Every Decision Counts

"It is in your moments of decision that your destiny is shaped."

Here's the plain and simple truth. Changes do not happen overnight. You can attain transformation, but you can't expect it to happen instantly. Success is a process. There is no one defining moment, but there is a lot of value in better choices done on a day-to-day basis.

Behind every habit, good or bad, is a series of small decisions made over the course of time. Most of the difficulties that we face were not born overnight. They came about as a consequence of hundreds, if not thousands, of bad choices we have made over time. In which case, the path to success is paved by thousands of daily good decisions that we can make over the course of years.

The key to becoming the person we want to be is not in the big defining moments. If you want to become more productive and be a better version of yourself, you should start paying more attention to the seemingly small and ordinary decisions that you make every single day. Habits come from these small choices.

New Decisions, New Life

"Your life changes the moment you make a new, congruent, and committed decision."

We are our habits. These are the things that come automatically to us. We are able to do them without thinking because they are deeply ingrained in our muscle memory. All habits, whether good or bad, begin in the same way. They are actions we do consciously. We do them over and over until they become an automatic part of us.

Be more conscious of the decisions that come automatically to you

Awareness or consciousness is the key here. Without awareness, it will be hard for you to realize the things that you must change in order to improve. Now there are certain actions that come automatically to us. However, if we take the time to ponder upon why we make these decisions or why we choose to do what we do, then we will have a chance to apply corrective actions.

For instance, you are used to having donuts with your coffee every morning. Why am I eating this instead of making eggs for breakfast? Is it because I lack the time? Is it because I am too lazy? What can I do to make more time in the morning? One question leads to another directing you to make better decisions.

Just Do It

"A real decision is measured by the fact that you've taken a new action. If there's no action, you haven't truly decided."

One of the things that make Tony Robbins such an effective motivational speaker is that he puts into practice the things that he teaches. He has a confidence and charisma that reflect in his work. These positive traits about him were not developed overnight. He understands that real decisions have to be acted upon.

Why unproductive habits are hard to break?
We find it incredibly easy to adopt an unhealthy set of routines. Some people bite their nails. Others develop a smoking habit. Most of us sleep late and go through a frantic rush in the morning. We binge on junk food, spend too much on non-essentials or laze around when we have tons of things to do. The list of unproductive and unhealthy behaviors seems endless. All of us struggle with these bad behaviors once in a

while.

The question is why do we fall into these unproductive habits when we truly want to live a productive and fruitful life? We experience spurts of inspiration to focus on our goals. Sometimes, we feel such a strong drive to take action. Unfortunately, we still spend most times doing the same things instead of exerting effort to do better. Why is it so easy to build habits than it is to stick to a few good ones?

It is probably because we are applying the wrong strategy. Perhaps we are trying so hard to change but we're doing it the wrong way. What is the right way? If you want things to change, you have to make a new decision and fully commit to it.

Consistency Is Key

"In essence, if we want to direct our lives, we must take control of our consistent actions. It's not what we do once in a while that shapes our lives, but what we do consistently."

Consistency builds habits. Practice over time reinforces habits. To be consistent, you need to practice patience because it will be your consistent habits that lead you to the path of success. With that said, the most challenging part is always the first few days and weeks. Now you know 66 days is the magic number for most, it is up to you to force the habit for this long until it becomes ingrained within.

Strive To Become The Person That Matches The Goal

"It's not about the goal. It's about growing to become the person that can accomplish that goal."

Goals are crucial at steering you in the right direction. They can give you a clear idea of the path you need to travel. However, focusing on your goals should not take away the focus from yourself.

There are a lot of important things Tony did to achieve success in the magnitude he has but there are 3 standouts:

Find a mentor

Tony had Jim Rohn to stir him in the right direction. Rohn provided him with invaluable knowledge to help Tony build and advance his own career. As soon as he decided on the route he wanted t take in life, he worked hard in preparing himself to upgrade his skill set. A combination of drive and the right attitude is essential..

Develop your personal brand

Tony Robbins used every medium at his disposal to get the word out about his work. He first became famous because of the infomercials he produced in order to sell his programs. He hosted seminars and wrote books. All these got him the recognition as a peak performance coach. He had one message and it was crystal clear.

Build your network

No one can do everything on his or her own. Everybody needs a support network. Tony Robbins used his charisma to build his. Throughout his career, he expanded his network. He interacted with other inspiring personalities like Princess Diana, Oprah Winfrey, François Mitterrand, Bill Clinton, Mikhail Gorbachev and Nelson Mandela among many others. In other words, he worked hard to become the person he needs to be to become worthy of his goals, the person who can achieve those goals.

You Are What You Repeatedly Do

"You become what you do most of the time."

Your life is essentially the sum of your habits. Whether you are productive or unproductive is because of the small decisions you make every day to do or not to do. You are healthy or unhealthy not because of one single huge choice but because of every small choice you have made over time that affects your lifestyle. It is because of your choice to or not to eat right or exercise. You are either happy or unhappy because of these "ordinary" choices.

We choose to succeed or fail every single moment. Our chance of succeeding or failing at something depends on the kind of habits we build, whether good or bad ones and this is why much more attention is needed on daily choices, habits and routines.

Problems Provide Growth

"Every problem is a gift–without problems we would not grow."

No one is immune to problems. Tony Robbins definitely had his share of difficulties. He went through everything from a failed marriage to media criticism, lawsuits and the like. As it turns out, even the most successful life coach in the world can't do all things perfectly. But what's most important is how you learn from your problems and take every lesson to grow as an individual.

Learn and let go

There are various kinds of problems. The first one is completely under your control. If it is, the best thing to do is find a reasonable resolution. The second one is not in your control but you may have influence over it and so you do your best to influence the outcome. If it doesn't work out, you have to be content with the fact that you exerted an effort.

The third and probably the most common one is completely

out of your control. You have no influence over it and the best thing to do is learn your lesson and move on. Avoid beating yourself up for the things you can do nothing about.

Give Back

"Only those who have learned the power of sincere and selfless contribution experience life's deepest joy: true fulfillment."

Although we may live separate lives, we are connected. We are intertwined. No one lives only for himself.

A truly fulfilling life is one that has meaning.
We create meaning beyond our own desires, wants and needs. To meet this need, it is crucial to recognize something greater than yourself. You bring meaning into your life when you learn to give without expecting anything in return, when you learn to share. Make an effort to contribute to other people's lives not for recognition. Learn to give without expectations of gain.

Making a difference is not easy.
Tony Robbins is a respected philanthropist. With his wealth and influence, he launched the 'Anthony Robbins Foundation'

in 1991. The foundation is dedicated to empowering students as well as prisoners by way of learning programs from Robbins' own teachings and food drives. He continues to dedicate himself to various charitable works.

Not everyone has the means to and you do not necessarily have to change the world. No one can do it on one's own. Inspire others with your selflessness. Have the courage for others to depend on. Making a difference enough to change the world may seem to be an impossible task, but you can certainly make a change in someone else's life in your own little way.

Use some of your time for volunteer work. If you have the means, contribute to charity. When a friend needs you, be there for him. Be supportive to your family. Show kindness to strangers. They may be small acts, but they can bring a deeper sense of fulfillment into your life.

Love Lends Meaning to Existence

"It's your unlimited power to care and to love that can make the biggest difference in the quality of your life."

There is nothing as powerful as the force of love. It can make you feel alive and complete, but the opposite is also true. Love can also cause the most unbearable pain a human being can experience.

People search for connections. We fulfill the need by building relationships. This is why some people dream of getting married. This is why we make friends. This is why we keep a dog.

There is nothing wrong with putting value in this need unless it causes you to overlook other needs or completely ignore them. If you do, you may lose your self-identity and become no one unless you're with that person. It is codependency.

In the same way, not putting importance to this need for love and connection can also render one's existence hollow and meaningless. With no one to share your life with, you may achieve the greatest height of success in your career or business but you may still feel empty inside.

Choose Wisely What To Believe

"Beliefs have the power to create and the power to destroy. Human beings have the awesome ability to take any experience of their lives and create a meaning that disempowers them or one that can literally save their lives."

What is it that you believe about yourself?

What do others believe about you?

A lot of people put more importance on the latter and that is when things get messy. The simple truth is that when it comes to your life, it has to be about you. You decide. You act. You choose what to believe in. DO not let others dictate your life.

Work on impressing yourself

Stop focusing on thinking about how to impress other people. The first person you need to impress is yourself. When you feel a sense of pride in your work, it shines through. You will be pleased with yourself. Nothing can compare to that feeling. Set the bar for yourself instead of waiting for others to set the standards. You have a hold of your motivation. The strongest drive is what comes from within you.

No Limits

"Our beliefs about what we are and what we can be precisely determine what we can be"

Our biggest enemy is ourselves. We impose self-limiting beliefs that drag us down instead of lifting us up. At the end of the day, we determine what we can be.

If Tony did not have the strength of character, he would not have managed to build a successful career. If he did not believe in himself, he would have remained a janitor his entire life. If he did not believe in himself, he would not have survived the many criticisms he faced throughout the years.

Decide

There is always a choice. You always have one. You can decide. Stop telling yourself, "I SHOULD", "I MUST" or "I HAVE TO." It may work but only to some extent. As a matter of fact, it is a sure way to weaken your drive. Instead, you can tell yourself, "I CHOOSE TO" or "MY DECISION IS TO DO THIS." Words are powerful. Choose to use positive ones.

Decide to use words that work for you.

Build on your strengths

Focusing on your weaknesses can be counterproductive. It will only diminish your drive. If you do think about them, do so objectively without emotional attachments. This way, you can work on finding ways to improve upon them. If you can't help but be worn down by your weaknesses, choose to focus on your strengths instead. This will help you find your flow and re-energize. With your strengths, you can be at your best and this can lead to building your momentum.

Know Your Target

"You can't hit a target if you don't know what it is."

Define your outcome. Begin at the end. You want to reach the top of a mountain? Visualize what is going to happen when you reach the end. How does it feel? What does it look and sound like? How does it smell and taste like?

Think of it as if you are planning your dream vacation. You have a destination in mind and you certainly have expectations on how you will feel when you get there. You know what you're going to see and hear. You can smell and taste it. A vision is just as real as any place in the world. If you define it with clarity and precision, you transform it from merely a thought in your head to something real and tangible.

Money Isn't Everything

"I think money makes people more of who they are. If you're mean, you've got more to be mean with. If you're giving, you've got more to give. It's a magnifying device. In today's world, it's nothing. It's ones and zeros."

If you have the means to, give back. Contribute to the improvement of other people's lives especially those who need help the most. Do your share.

For Tony, it is not just about giving away money. It is adding value to other people's lives. He has the knowledge and resources. Being the true philanthropist that he is, he makes an effort to share both his knowledge and resources to make a contribution.

"You either master money, or, on some level, money masters you."

Some people are so obsessed with making money that they spend most of their lives building their wealth. It seems as if their value as people is defined by the number of zeros in their bank account, the size of their house and all their properties. They are too busy making money that they do not realize there are other more important things in life.

"And always remember the ultimate truth: life is not about money, it's about emotion."
Money may define the quality of your living. However, it does not define the quality of your life. When we die, people we have left behind will not remember us for how much money we made. Is it the kind of legacy you want to leave behind? Your entire existence defined in numbers.
NO. People will remember us for how we were as a person, how we treated those around us, how we lived if we truly did. Focus on what is inside you. Strive for a goal not because of money but by the sense of pride and fulfillment it gives you because it is something you are truly passionate about.

Use Emotion For Motivation

"Lack of emotion causes lack of progress and lack of motivation."

Emotions are not all bad. Emotions can cloud our judgment but when used properly, they can also become an endless source of motivation. Tony and other successful people have mastered the power of emotions and used them to their best advantage. They are not only looking at the goals. They also understand the reason behind those goals. They feel strongly about it.

Figure out your personal why

Why do you want what you want? What is the reason behind vision? Why is your mission important to you?

In times of hardship, your personal why will help you push through. When you are losing it, your personal why will give you hope. When you are not feeling like it, your personal why will drive you to action. Asking yourself why will help you clearly understand why you are doing what it is that you need

---

to do.

Follow Your Passion

"There is no greatness without a passion to be great, whether it's the aspiration of an athlete or an artist, a scientist, a parent, or a businessperson."

If you do not feel passionate about something, you will never find enough motivation to be great at it. People like Tony Robbins figured out what they are passionate about and that is what made them push themselves to achieve great things.

Figure out your purpose

Find your purpose and make it compelling. This is why you need to figure out a purpose that is bigger than yourself. This is what will keep you going.

And if it calls for it, you also need the strength to evaluate your personal reasons, your purpose. At times, we do not get it right the first time. We may be doing the right things but for the wrong reasons. Are you simply completing a task and getting things done? Or are you learning something new? Are you growing? If you make your purpose compelling enough, it will ignite a fire within you.

Create More Than You Consume

"You have to make the shift from being a consumer in the economy to becoming an owner—and you do it by becoming an investor."

Tony Robbins does not only write about relationships, persuasive communication, health and energy and pushing through fears. His book "Awaken the Giant Within" which was published in 1991 is about taking care of one's physical, emotional as well as financial destiny. "Money: Master the Game", which happens to be his third bestseller book, delved into wealth insights guided by his collaboration and interviews with more than 50 financial experts.

Invest in something

Whether it is about investing in stocks, properties or yourself, you have to make it a point to invest in something. Do not just consume. Aspire to become an influencer, and being an influencer means making a commitment in the form of investment into something.

This is not just about money

There are various things you can invest in and you can also invest in people. Why not invest in yourself? Pursue higher education. Take an online course. Learn and develop new skills. Do things necessary to prepare you to become the person you want to be and achieve the things you desire.

Set The Standard

"If you don't set a baseline standard for what you'll accept in life, you'll find it's easy to slip into behaviors and attitudes or a quality of life that's far below what you deserve."

Most people are content with merely going with the flow. Sometimes, we have no choice but to go with the flow. However, if we have a choice, we must choose to act according to our personal standards.

The likes of Tony Robbins who have achieved great success in their chosen field have decided on an acceptable standard for themselves. It is this standard that guides their decisions and behaviors. Through their standards, they avoid falling astray from the path they have chosen for themselves. Most importantly, they have decided on these standards. They do not let others dictate them.

"Your income right now is a result of your standards, it is not the industry; it is not the economy."

This standard extends to income. Therefore, if you are earning so little and working too hard, you cannot blame it all on the economy. Part of it should be blamed on yourself. Why? You have set that standard and you have accepted it. Otherwise, you will strive harder to get the income you feel you deserve.

Connect to your values

You need to find a connection between the things you want and your personal values. As long as you are fully connected to your values, you will always make an effort to work towards achievement. So, what do you value? Which do you feel most connected to?

If you value learning and growth, you do not just say, "I am getting things done." Instead, you say, "I am learning something new." If you value contribution, do not just say, "doing a favor." Rather, you should say "adding value to." If you value love and connection, you do not say "hanging out." Instead, you should say "making a connection."

Even small changes in your choice of words can help strengthen your resolve. It will change your perspective or how you look at things. It will change how you feel about what you do. Tasks are not just things you have to do anymore. You will begin to see tasks as opportunities.

Find Your Meaning

"Things do not have meaning. We assign meaning to everything."

What may mean something to you may not be as important to another. A watch is just another watch like a million other watches to me, but that watch may mean the world to you. It may symbolize something more meaningful. It could have been given to you as a parting gift or an heirloom.

Things are just things. What Tony Robbins wants us to understand in this quote is that we choose which things have meaning to us, therefore, it is necessary for us to choose carefully.

Follow Pareto

The Pareto Principle, also known as the 80/20 rule points out a fact that most of us may not realize and that is - everything is not equal. It is a waste of our efforts to treat them as equals. Causes and results are not balanced. Just because you give 50 percent does not necessarily mean you will receive 50 percent.

The key here is to find the strong 20 percent and focus on them.

The reality is a majority creates little to zero impact on one hand. On the other side is the small minority that accounts for major impact. So how do we apply the Pareto Principle to our daily lives and maximize our effectiveness and efficiency?

It's simple. Drill down to the basics to find the things or people that are truly essential and focus on them. They may be so few. But at the end of the day, it is these essentials that truly give your life meaning.

Determination

"The path to success is to take massive, determined action."

The path to success is long and winding. Tony Robbins can attest to that. Nobody takes a shortcut. There are ups and downs and curve balls. Challenges do not end. They continue to make things difficult and all it requires of you to make it through is enough determination.

Progress cannot be forced. It is never instant. It requires time and effort. You need to be patient. As you put in the work towards mastery, you see one small bit of progress at a time. As these small wins build up, it will eventually become exponential.

Be Patient

It is possible for you to hit a plateau. It does not mean you have to stop trying. It does not mean you have to quit. It does not mean you have maximized the results of your efforts. You need to push through and keep going. It may require a bit of change in your strategy or more effort, but the key is to keep pushing forward until you see compounding returns.

Keep going

Once you hit momentum, keep building it up. This is only possible if you keep doing, if you keep acting, if you keep exerting effort. Motivation to start is crucial but the motivation to keep doing is what fuels a self-fulfilling cycle. So do not stop. Do not quit. Keep moving forward and pushing harder until you experience the results you are targeting. It will eventually happen. You have to believe that.

Inspiration

"The secret to unleashing your true power is setting goals that are exciting enough that they truly inspire your creativity and ignite your passion."

Tony Robbins encourages us to find something inspiring to hold on to. Motivation to do something worthwhile wouldn't last unless we feel strongly about it, unless we are passionate about it.

If Tony was not determined enough. He would have given up after the originality of his first book "Unlimited Power" was disputed. It was a bittersweet experience. Although the book published in 1987 made it to the bestseller list, some people questioned the originality of his ideas presented in the book, but he had a vision and he remained committed to it.

Connect to your vision

Everyone dreams. Unpleasant experiences silence our ability to dream. Reality can numb us and push us to bury our dreams. Dig deep and find yours. Hope comes from clear vision. Vision defines your life's purpose. It is your vision that will bring meaning to your existence. Otherwise, you will end up just coasting through life. Getting yourself to developing your vision statement can be the big leap. It will turn your life around!

Vision paints the big picture. Goals are the fine pigments. Without these fine pigments, the picture will not be complete. Vision draws the framework which you can use to define your goals and you can use them to guide every decision you make and every action you take.

Do It For Yourself, NOT For Recognition

"It's what you practice in private that you will be rewarded for in public."

There are plenty of things people do not know about the works of Tony Robbins. What is presented is this self-help guru that garnered massive success in his field. Nobody truly knows the process and hardship he went through to receive that status. He may be known as a philanthropist but not all his charitable works are publicized. Nevertheless, he continues with his work. He does not stop striving to help other people through his work.

Do not strive for recognition

What the right hand does need not be known by the left hand. A lot of people are obsessed about getting a nod from others. They try so hard to please other people. However, the only person you need to please is yourself. Do not live by their standards. Set your own and live by them.

Work on impressing yourself

Even little efforts deserve commendation. All your little efforts to improve on yourself are significant. It may be a tiny dot in the big picture. However, without the tiny dots, the picture won't be complete.

Focus on intrinsic motivation

Motivation and drive are either intrinsic or extrinsic. Internal drive comes from within. This is the kind of reward that is within you. This is why people do things that make them feel good. This is also why personal satisfaction and connecting with your personal values is important.

Extrinsic motivation, on the other hand, is the kind of rewards that are externalized. A few examples include a tap on the back, a sign of approval from other people or something of the material kind. This is why rewarding yourself with a shopping spree, a vacation or a new car helps.

Drive that comes from outside is helpful but relying on them alone may not be wise. If you have to choose which side to lean on, you should be more dependent on internal drive and you can do this by fully committing to your purpose and connecting to your values.

Live Life

"Live life fully while you're here. Experience everything. Take care of yourself and your friends. Have fun; be crazy; be weird. Go out and screw up! You're going to anyway, so you might as well enjoy the process."

Nobody is capable of doing things perfectly, not the first, second or hundredth time. The simple truth is that nobody is perfect.

Tony Robbins seem like he is living the ideal life. He has money. He is famous and he has the respect of people. However, he is far from perfect. His personal life is not ideal. His first marriage failed. He has children from different mothers and that is the key takeaway in this quote. We all make mistakes.

Allow yourself to make mistakes

Stop beating yourself up for everything. You are and can never be perfect. You are human and you are bound to make mistakes. Cut yourself some slack. However, try your best to avoid making the same mistake twice or more.

Live outside the box

Do not constraint yourself. Let loose. You have freedom. Live freely and happily the best possible way you can.

Stay true to who you are

Never compromise your self-identity. You are at your happiest when you are true to yourself. Celebrate your uniqueness. Bask in your weirdness.

Take risks

Most rewards come after taking a risk. Do not be content with what is comfortable and safe. You have to allow yourself to wander into the world and explore other possibilities. That is the only way you can truly enjoy life. Do not stop learning. Start and enjoy living.

15 Success Principles To Live By

This is a list of what I believe to be Tony's most powerful lessons he has taught us. I like to go over this list every morning at the end of my priming session. Once engrained in your mind, these nuggets of wisdom will positively impact the decisions and choices you make every day.

Repetition is key

Anything worth achieving doesn't come easy. To achieve the hard things in life it takes constant, daily action. Beating on your craft day in day out. If you want it badly enough you will force yourself into action even on the days you really don't feel like it. Repetition is truly the mother of skill.

Where focus goes energy flows

Following on suitably from point one, whatever we focus on

in life will undoubtedly grow. This can go either way though. Focus on ways to add value to the world or yourself and that will happen. Focus on why you can't achieve something and guess what will happen? We can get better at this by questioning ourselves and finding out what it is we really want. When we get to the bottom of that, that will drive our focus and the energy will swiftly follow.

Figure out the "what" and the "why" and the "how" will reveal itself

Linking nicely again to the point above, you may already know what you want but are unsure of how to get there. Keep focusing your energy towards this goal ensuring your why is so big you become unstoppable. With this type of focus and drive, your 'how' will soon reveal itself.

Results beat activity

Huge to-do-lists may keep you busy but there's a difference

between busyness and effectiveness. Once you have a clear idea of exactly the results you wish to achieve you'll become more efficient and effective on your journey to achieving it. Develop a results-focused, purpose driven, massive action plan and follow it.

Resources are not the problem

They may make it a struggle but plenty of people have succeeded with much worst odds. Start small and focus on steady growth whilst becoming more resourceful. Today more information and opportunity is available than ever before due in large part to the Internet. Utilize it. Create more than you consume. Remember, Tony started his path leaving home at 17 with no college education working as a janitor.

Define yourself wisely

Have you ever sat down and taken the time to seriously think about the person you want to be? If not, do it. Now practice being that person every day no matter how uncomfortable it may feel at first. This is who you will eventually see yourself as and so will everyone else. By making small mindful decisions every day, you can re-define yourself.

If you're in your head, you're dead

Get out of your head and into your body, passion and energy. When you are low on energy your head takes over and that's when fear sets in. Find out what gets you going whenever you feel a lull approaching. This could include incantations, motivational videos or some upbeat music. These will make you feel alive, playful and fully appreciating the moment without worries for the future.

Progress comes from smashing through your self-imposed limiting beliefs

Whether you are aware of this or not, your limiting beliefs are holding you back. The only way you can change this is by being truly honest with yourself and listing any fears that are stopping you from achieving your goals. Once listed, ask yourself if you are 100% certain that you can't push past this. Rarely does anything in life come with 100% certainty so now it's time to get creative and truly figure out how you can smash through your previous belief system.

A 2 mm change is sometimes all you need

Sometimes the smallest changes can produce outstanding results. All areas of life can be optimized and you can apply this to your business, health, relationships and finances. If you're nearly there but just keep slightly missing the mark, a tweak here and there can make all the difference. Just don't give up!

The fastest way to change your story is to change your state

The story you tell yourself every day about the person you are is just that – a story. We all know how our perception changes dependent on the mood we are in. How do you improve this story? By changing your emotions and improving your state. The fastest way to do this is to move and shock the body. Whether this is through exercise, cold exposure, heat exposure, dancing, singing, the list is endless and it is completely up to you!

Body language

Another useful method for mastering out emotional states with our body is to be consciously aware of our body language. If you're standing tall with your chest out, shoulders back and chin up you're much more likely to feel more self assured and confident.

Contrast that with the image with being slumped over, head down and avoiding eye contact you are much more likely to feel as bad as you look. Controlling your physiology is key. This may require more concentrated effort at first but eventually it will become a habit and therefore natural.

Gratitude is key

We've already gone over this is the priming chapter but it is so important I thought worth mentioning again. Trade your expectations for appreciation and your life will improve significantly.

3 Mandates of Leadership

To be an effective leader we need to follow the 3 mandates of leadership.

• See things as they are, not worse than they are.

• You need to see things better than they are. Provide a vision.

• Make it the way you now see it. Lead the way into making the vision a reality.

Decisions lead to destiny

Our circumstances don't define us, the decisions we make do. Every decision we make either leads us one step closer or further away from our goals. There are three decisions we make both consciously and subconsciously: what am I going to focus on? What does it mean to me? What am I going to do about it? Choose these answers wisely and chase down your destiny.

Proximity is power

Tony's mentor Jim Rohn said it best: "You are the average of the five people you spend the most time with." Choose the people you surround yourself with carefully.

Conclusion

It would be hard to argue that Tony Robbins is the greatest success coach in the world. Through his books, videos, presenting seminars and workshops around the world he has impacted the lives of millions. The "Michael Jordan" of thought leaders, it seems he is only just getting started with his popularity growing by the year. I hope this book has helped not only motivate you, but to present the idea of instilling small daily habits for massive long-term results. I wish you the best of luck on your journey.

Thanks for checking out my book. I hope you found this of value and enjoyed it. But before you go, I have one small favor to ask…

Would you take 60 seconds and write a quick blurb about this book on Amazon?

Reviews are the best way for independent authors (like me) to get noticed, sell more books, and it gives me the motivation to continue producing. I also read every review and use the feedback to write future revisions – and even future books. Thanks again.

67096275R00058

Made in the USA
Lexington, KY
01 September 2017